enjoying
GYMNASTICS

enjoying GYMNASTICS

by the **DIAGRAM GROUP**

PADDINGTON PRESS LTD

*Dedicated to the children of Paddington Press
and the Diagram Group*

Library of Congress Cataloging in Publication Data
Diagram Group.
   Enjoying gymnastics.

   Includes index.
   1. Gymnastics.   I. Title.
   GV461.D48   1976   796.4'1   76-3810
   ISBN 0-8467-0141-3

In the USA Paddington Press Ltd
In the UK Paddington Press Ltd
In Canada Distributed by
          Random House of Canada Ltd

© **Diagram Visual Information Ltd** 1976
Editor Christopher C. Pick
Associate editor David Heidenstam
Research editor Ruth Berenbaum
Artists Jim Kane, Richard Hummerstone, Robert Galvin, Anne and Jane Robertson
Consultants Nick Stewart, MBE, Olympic gymnastics coach
          Susan Ogle, gymnastics coach for children aged from 12 to 18 years
          Judit Kertesz, gymnastics coach for children aged up to 12 years

Foreword

Gymnastics is one of the purest of all sporting activities, proving the human body capable of movements and forms of the greatest beauty. In his or her actions the gymnast expresses rhythms and shapes that are the basis of music, art, and architecture. When we watch a successful gymnast it is as though we are seeing the true function of the human frame.

From the smile of a child viewing the world upside down in a handstand to the delicate, alert poise of an Olympic competitor about to start a complicated sequence, this book encompasses the full joy of gymnastics.

Throughout the book a profusion of illustrations, supported by an explanatory text, captures the excitement of gymnastics. The first chapter describes the simplest activities and typical equipment. The second explains competition exercises and how events are judged. The third illustrates sports and pastimes in which gymnastic skills are used. The fourth offers easy exercises which can be practiced at home. The final section contains a glossary to help readers with unfamiliar terms.

The editors are particularly grateful to the sports' coaches who assisted in the production of this book. We hope that we have conveyed their enthusiasm and that their advice will encourage even more young people to start *enjoying gymnastics*.

Contents

Pages of a German manual of
gymnastics published in 1845.

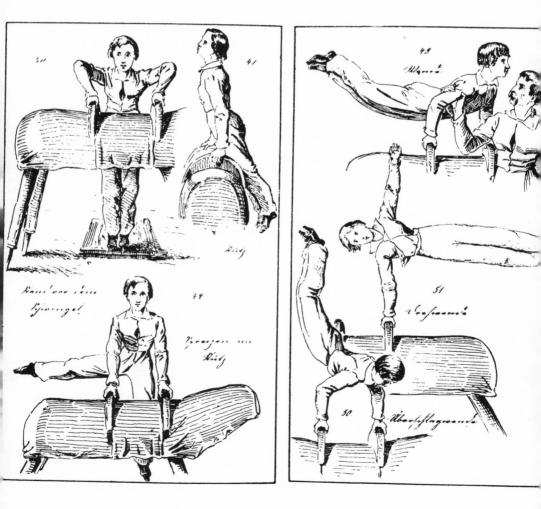

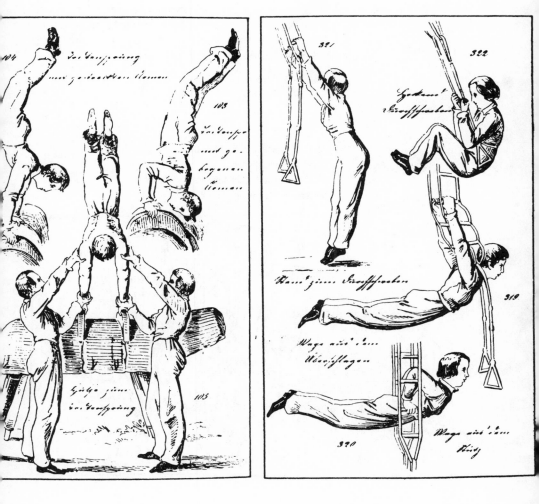

Gymnastics is both an exciting and a beautiful sport. It not only demands physical courage from those who take part, but grace and mastery of the body as well.

This book will show you how to begin training to be a gymnast. It isn't necessary to be a second Olga Korbut to keep yourself physically fit, and everyone should be able to do some of the simple exercises described later on. Persevere with these and you will be surprised how soon you will be able to go on to more difficult ones.

Because gymnastics isn't just a matter of fabulous tricks high in the air, it is necessary to understand the principles on which the human body works and can be controlled. Only with such knowledge will you be able to develop the special qualities that mark out the really top-class gymnast.

An early depiction of a gymnastic display. In any age, the professional performer depends on perfect balance and control.

To achieve perfect poise the body must be balanced. The point around which a body is balanced is known as its center of gravity. This point can be inside or outside the body – depending on the body's position. But there is always an equal amount of body weight on either side of it.

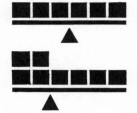

The turning body always rotates around an axis, whether it is moving forward or backward, spinning, or rotating left or right.

Side axis gives forward-backward motion.

Vertical axis gives spin.

Front-back axis gives side motion.

The movements of the body

The human body is tough and yet delicate at the same time. This is not as contradictory as it seems. It is tough because it can take far more strain than most people ever put on it and can be exercised far more vigorously than they ever attempt. But it is also a delicate instrument which has to be handled carefully: don't expect to be able to do difficult exercises without a great deal of training and practice. Follow the advice of a gym instructor or a knowledgeable adult and train regularly, gradually building up to the really exciting and skillful feats. That way you will do yourself no harm.

Below and on the opposite page we show some of the ranges of movement for the parts of the body most used in gymnastics.

neck

spine, forward-backward

spine, sideways

shoulders

hips

knees, ankles

To start training as a gymnast all you really need is a reasonably large floor space covered by a mat or carpet. On this you can practice simple rolls, handstands, somersaults, etc. and begin to exercise your muscles regularly. Soon, though, you will need to use special gymnastic equipment for the more difficult exercises and to develop different parts of your body. Don't use furniture at home for this: apart from the fact that you will probably damage it, you may harm yourself as well—after all, chairs aren't made to be vaulted over!

On this and the following pages are illustrated some of the most important pieces of gymnastic equipment. Most, if not all, of these you will find in your school or club gymnasium. It is there, with the help of instructors, that you should do most of your serious training. What you can do at home is to follow a regular pattern of keep-fit exercises. A few minutes when you get up in the morning and before you go to bed will do a lot to keep your body alert and supple. Turn to page 136 for suggestions for keep-fit exercises to do at home.

Wherever you train, one of the best pieces of equipment is a large mirror, so that you can see what you are doing and judge your progress. Start by standing in front of it and seeing how still you can make your body.

Gymnasts start most exercises standing on the floor. Sometimes however they have to use a springboard—usually when they are required to do a jump immediately.

vaulting horse

springboard

ladder   wall and bars   rope ladder   rope

medicine ball   skipping rope   indian clubs   ribbon

bench

Gymnastic equipment

Drawings from an Italian print of the 18th century show a small boy playing with a hoop and pole.

Although gymnastics were only officially recognized late in the 19th century, the gymnast's skills have been practiced since before classical times.

The side or pommel horse has two handles, known as pommels. These are grasped by the gymnasts as they maneuver or vault over the horse.

For vaults done along the length of the horse, the pommels are removed and the horse's height is usually increased.

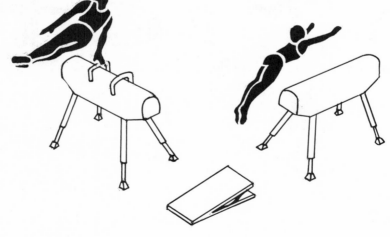

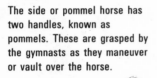

This is the gymnasium in the sports school in Grodno, USSR, where Olga Korbut started on the path to her gold medal. Notice the large mirror on the wall and the thick padding on the floor.

The beam is one of the most demanding pieces of equipment. On it, skills difficult enough when performed on the ground have to be mastered several feet in the air.

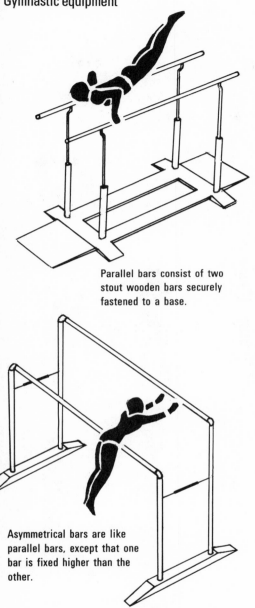

Parallel bars consist of two stout wooden bars securely fastened to a base.

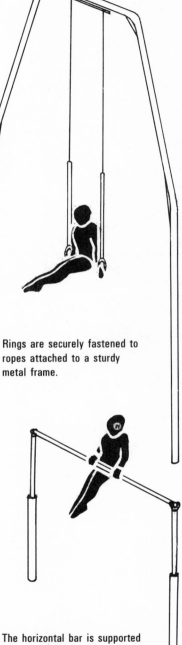

Rings are securely fastened to ropes attached to a sturdy metal frame.

Asymmetrical bars are like parallel bars, except that one bar is fixed higher than the other.

A competitor performing on the parallel bars during the 1968 Olympic Games in Mexico City.

The horizontal bar is supported on two steel uprights.

When exercising in the gym, it is essential that suitable clothing be worn for both comfort and safety. The choice of what to wear often depends upon the activity, but there are certain rules that should always be observed. For instance, long hair can be a problem when performing activities such as the bridge or forward roll, and it should therefore be tied back into a pony-tail or pig-tails or held in place with a headband. The correct choice of footwear is also essential and once again can depend upon the activity. Sneakers, stockings, and bare feet are all permissible, but shoes should never be worn, even if you are not performing, as they can cause irreparable damage to a gym floor.

Finally, if you are considering becoming more seriously involved in gymnastics, it is a good idea to have a tracksuit which will keep you warm while watching others or waiting your turn.

leotard,
stretch trousers and vest

pants and vest,
overalls and vest

leg warmers,
footless tights

one piece and two piece
tracksuits

Exercises with a partner

On this and the following pages we describe how to do some of the simplest gymnastic exercises. You can do most of them at home, either indoors or in the yard; you can also try them in the park or, if you are on vacation, on the beach.

Follow the instructions very carefully. If you are not sure what to do, ask your gym instructor at school or any adult. Trying it on your own isn't clever: it can lead to serious physical damage, possibly even to a spell in the hospital. Get someone to help you the first few times you do the exercises. He will guide you and help to correct your mistakes.

The exercises on this page and the next also need the help of a partner. If you try them out with a friend, remember that both of you must be sure of yourselves. Not everyone may be as good at gymnastics as you are!

high kicking
Get your partner to hold his arm out in front of him. Then kick your foot up and see if you can reach his hand. If you can, get him to hold it higher. Gradually increase height. Do not let other leg bend as you kick.

topsy-turvy walk
Do a handstand and get your partner to grasp your ankles. At the same time take hold of his feet. Then walk together.

high leap frog
Stand with your arms to your sides, slightly bending your shoulders and tucking your head forward. Get your partner to take a run-up of 2 or 3 steps and leap over you, pressing his hands down on your shoulders.

backward roll over back

Get your partner to put his
head between your legs. Then
lean back until you can both
grasp each other's shoulders.
As your partner straightens up
toward the standing position,
look backward and kick your
legs over his head. Finish
standing straight.

back to back toss

Stand back to back with your
partner and grasp each other's
hands above your shoulders.
Then bend forward and lift your
partner up, so that he rolls
over your shoulders and lands
facing you in a standing
position.

slow flick-flack

Stand back to back with your
partner and grasp each other's
hands above your shoulders.
Then bend over toward the
floor, so your partner rests on
your back. Return to standing,
then rest back on your partner
as he bends forward.

The movements set out in this and the next five pages are all basic gymnastic exercises. Many can be done not only on the floor but also on horses, bars, rings, and beams. To be a successful gymnast you must master them.

Ideally, you should try these exercises out on a proper mat in the gymnasium. If that isn't possible, some of the simple ones can be done on a carpet at home. Try to keep within an area about 12 meters square, because that is the size allowed in competitions, and part of a gymnast's skill is in not going off the edge of the mat.

Don't rush things. However attractive somersaults and flips may look, you won't be able to control your body well enough to do them properly until you have mastered the basic skills —handstands, rolls, and cartwheels.

Remember that gymnastics is a graceful sport. Your movements should be smooth and your body quite still when you start and finish.

forward roll
With feet together and knees bent, crouch and lower hands to floor, tucking head between arms. Straighten legs and push from toes so that you roll forward onto back of neck. Keep body tucked in and roll over onto feet, pushing arms forward to help momentum.

backward roll
Squat down, with arms at shoulder level, hands palm up, head tucked forward. Move backward, bringing seat to floor, and immediately roll back onto back and shoulders. When toes touch mat behind, press hands hard against floor to come out into squat or standing position.

headstand

Squat with hands on floor, shoulder width apart. Place forehead on mat 12 in. in front of fingertips. Straighten legs and pull hips up and over shoulders, extending legs toward ceiling. Keep seat tucked in and stomach tight.

handstand

With hands straight above head, take long step forward and bend front leg, keeping arms in line with body. As hands reach toward floor, kick back leg up to vertical; when hands have reached floor, push up front leg.

To descend, bring one leg down, keeping the other vertical. As first leg reaches floor, push hard on hands to bring body to vertical, keeping arms raised above head. Keep your body straight. Hands must be straight above head, and there must be no angle between arms and shoulders.

Don't lift your head as you reach the handstand, or you will have to arch your back to maintain balance.

handstand and forward roll

Complete handstand. Then bend arms, tuck head between arms and lower shoulders, keeping rest of body straight. Roll body forward to sitting position with legs bent and arms stretched out, ready to stand up.

handspring (far right)
Start as for handstand.
Once legs are in air, keep head back, shoulders forward, and legs straight. As legs pass through handstand position, thrust hard with hands. Land on balls of feet, with knees slightly bent. Straighten to standing position.

headspring (above)
Put forehead on floor in front of hands and spring up to angle headstand, keeping legs at right angle to body. Let hips fall forward and swing legs up, pushing hard with hands. Stretch out whole body as high as possible as you leap. Land on toes, knees bent, arms out.

forward walkover (above)
Start as for handstand. Kick back leg up, then front leg, until body is inverted and legs in split position. Let lead leg continue down to floor. When ball of lead foot reaches floor, push body upright but keep other leg in air parallel to floor.

Remember to extend body fully as you start walkover (1) and to keep back arched as you bring second leg down (2).

flyspring or dive handspring (above)

Run up, leap high with arms above head and descend onto hands, taking legs through handstand position. Finish as for handspring, pushing hard with hands, stretching body, and landing on toes, with knees bent and arms out.

forward somersault (below)

Start as for flyspring. At top of jump, lift hips up and pull knees to a tucked position, grasping the shins. Pull shoulders and chest in. Hold until $\frac{3}{4}$ circle in air completed, then lift head and arms and stretch body ready to land. If you find yourself falling, go into forward roll.

Do not attempt this exercise without safety mats and expert supervision.

back extension roll

Sit on floor. Lean back and swing arms over head, placing them on floor next to ears. As you roll onto upper back, shoot legs up vertically, while pushing hands against floor as in handstand position.

backward walkover

With arms above head, lift one leg as high as possible, then bend body back, raising leg further. Put both hands on floor and bring first leg through vertical so that legs are in wide splits position. As first leg descends to floor, push with hands to return body to vertical, stretching arms overhead and holding second leg horizontally behind body.

back handspring

From standing position, bend knees, swing arms back, lean back, and force body up into air, bringing feet together. Extend arms and bring body through handstand position, raising head and shoulders as legs descend. Finish by standing with arms above head. Do not attempt this exercise without safety mats and expert supervision.

backward somersault

From standing position with arms above head, bend knees and lower arms; then thrust arms up and jump, pushing feet into ground for maximum thrust. Stretch body as high as possible and throw head back as toes leave floor, tucking knees into chest and grasping thighs with arms. Hold until turn $\frac{3}{4}$ complete; then let go of arms and legs to descend to floor.
Do not attempt this exercise without safety mats and expert supervision.

Vaulting

You will need a gymnasium to try out the ideas on this and the next three pages. Don't be too confident at first: it may look easy, but quite a lot of skill is involved. It's sensible to get somebody to help you the first time you try something out. With their advice you will improve much more quickly.

Vaulting, shown on this page and the next, is one of the oldest gymnastic skills, though many of the most exciting feats have only been introduced recently. As with all gymnastic exercises, master the basics—the squat and straddle vaults —before you attempt the more difficult exercises.

handspring over horse
Remove pommels from horse. Take off from springboard with both legs and land with hands on side of horse. Kick legs up and over, arching back and holding head up. Push off with arms and shoulders. Land on mat with arms out.

squat vault (above)
Run up and extend body as you take off, extending arms toward horse. Push hands firmly down on pommels as you vault over, tucking knees in and keeping back straight. Extend legs again ready to land.

stride vault (far right)
Run up and take off as in squat vault. With hands on pommels swing rear leg over horse, releasing hands briefly. Then bring other leg over in

same way, straighten body, and push off from horse with hands. Land on balls of feet, with knees bent, and finish standing straight.

flank vault (above top)
Stand with hands on horse to each side of body. Take off on both feet, swinging feet to one side and placing body weight on hand on opposite side. As legs clear horse, push off with support hand. Land with knees partly bent and arms stretched out.

face vault (above center)
Start as for flank vault. Take off on both feet and make $\frac{1}{4}$ turn above horse so that body passes above length of horse, parallel to it. Land alongside horse with one hand on it, the other stretched out sideways.

wolf vault (above)
Stand with hands on horse and legs apart. Swing leg above horse as for flank vault, bending other leg up under buttocks. Land with legs apart and arms stretched sideways.

cross-legs climbing (1, 2)
Raise right foot so that rope passes over leg below knee and above ankle (1). Pull up and cross left leg over right (2). Press legs together and lie back with straight arms to rest, then continue climbing by pushing with legs and moving hands above one another.

stand on rope (3, 4)
Bending knees, hips, and arms, stand on rope, with one foot above rope, the other beneath (3). Climb by extending hips and knees and moving hands up rope (4).

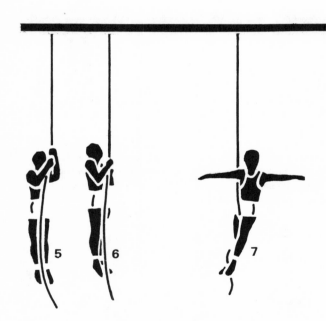

climbing with hands only (5, 6)
With body and legs straight, move hands up rope in small steps, keeping arms bent and hands just above chin. Descend in the same way. Don't slide, or you will scorch your hands.

making fast (7)
Stand on rope with feet above one another and rope running between them, behind one leg, and between the thighs. Stretch arms out and press back so that rope runs behind arms and over side of body.

chin position (1, 2)
Raise arms and grasp rings,
Bending elbows, pull body up
so that face is level with rings,
keeping legs straight and
pointing toes.
If necessary, to build up
strength at first, get someone
to help to lift you.

body circle (3)
Grasp rings. Keeping toes on
mat and legs straight, move
body through full circle.

swing in chin position (4)
Pull body up and bring face
level to rings. Extend lower
part of body and legs slightly
and swing gently from waist,
keeping legs straight and toes
pointed.

upstart position (5)
Grasp rings, which should be at
shoulder height. Kick one leg
up and back, then second leg,
flexing arms as body rotates
back to piked position. In piked
position, keep legs and arms
straight, toes pointed, and do
not over-rotate.

inverted hang (6)
From completed upstart
position, slowly straighten
body, keeping legs straight and
toes pointed. Continue until
body is perpendicular to floor,
with back slightly arched, and
hold.

The first need of a gymnast is to be supple and strong. These qualities are not only essential for performing the various exercises successfully and without strain but also bring grace and beauty to the sport.

Never attempt the suppling and strengthening exercises when your body is cold at the beginning of a session in the gym. Always warm up first, for at least half an hour. Be careful too that you get in the correct posture for each exercise; otherwise severe harm may result.

leg exercises
Lift each leg as far forward, backward, and sideways as possible. Keep supporting leg straight, with heel on ground, and back and head up. Do not twist hips. Get a fellow gymnast to support you. He may also help a little by giving constant *slow* pressure.

With body stretched out horizontally and supporting leg straight, stretch leg as high as possible, for as long as possible. Your partner should let go after a few seconds.

Kneel on ground with arms straight, head up, and body parallel to floor. Lift leg up and back as high as possible, keeping it straight all the time. Repeat with other leg.

splits

Splits should be practiced on both legs, increasing leg range as much as possible while stretching the body forward and backward.

bridge position

From lying position, bend elbows and place hands on floor by ears. Bend knees. Push hands and feet against floor until body is in bridge position. Press hips down so shoulders go beyond hands; relax; repeat.

back flexibility

Lie flat on stomach. For lower back, partner straddles legs, leans forward, grasps hands, and gently pulls body from floor.

For upper back, partner straddles shoulders, leans forward, grasps ankles, and gently pulls hips from floor.

In each case, partner should lift up and back—*not* straight back.

Flexibility and strength in
partnership.

Safety in the gym

This comic strip shows just one example of the accidents that can happen in gymnasiums. Never do anything in a gym without supervision—even though you may have the best of intentions. Be careful and sensible, listen to your instructor, and don't try anything that you have not been shown how to do. With proper supervision and discipline, the gym is a safe, but still exciting, place. Without them, it can be dangerous. Of course, playing outdoors needs care and commonsense, too. Gym equipment will not fail you, as a tree or a wall or a cliff face might do. But it has to be used properly.

39

A stone monument to a Greek
gymnast erected in Athens in
the 5th century BC.

Competitive gy

42

8ᶜ

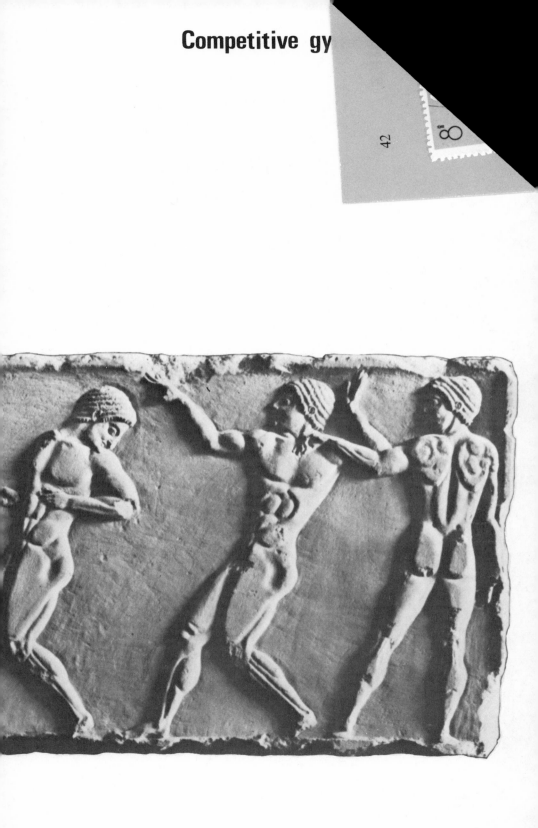

Man has always been a gymnast, for he has always understood the value to his mental and physical health of regular exercise and has always appreciated the beauty of skillful and elegant movement of the body.

Gymnastics first became popular in Ancient Greece, where amid the soft pine woods of Olympia gymnasts and athletes gathered every four years to compete in the famous Games. In Ancient Rome, too, such contests were held. Then, though men still valued physical prowess and courage, gymnastics as such virtually vanished until the nineteenth century, when, in the 1820s and 1830s, Ludwig Jahn founded gym clubs *(Turnverein)* throughout Germany. He also developed much of the equipment still in use today, including the parallel bars, horizontal bar, rings, and the horse. These clubs were both recreational and patriotic in intent, for Jahn believed fervently in the value of physical exercise and also wanted to develop healthy and well-trained citizens able to fight for their country. After that, rapid progress was made: the first gym club in the United States was founded in 1850, the first training college for gymnastics teachers fifteen years later, and in 1888 the Amateur Gymnastics Association was formed in Great Britain.

Gymnastics was one of the seven sports included in the first modern Olympic Games, held in Athens in 1896. Since then it has become more and more popular. Women's gymnastic events were introduced in the 1928 Olympics, and since 1950 a world championship has been held every four years. Most important, however, has been the ever-increasing number of gymnasts training in schools and clubs throughout the world and the official recognition that the sport has been given, especially in Russia and Eastern Europe.

There are three distinct gymnastic competitions in the Olympics and in world championship events: a team competition, an individual combined events competition, and individual events competitions. In the first of these, the team competition, the six members of each national team perform a compulsory and an optional exercise on each piece of apparatus. In the individual combined events competition, the top 36 gymnasts in the team competition each perform an optional exercise on each piece of apparatus. For the individual events competitions, the six best competitors on each piece of apparatus in the team competition are required to compete again for individual titles. Medals are awarded to the victorious countries in the team competition, to the individual victors in the individual combined events competition and to the victors on each piece of apparatus in the individual events competitions.

Women competitors perform on the vaulting horse, beam, asymmetrical bars and floor, men on the vaulting horse, pommel horse, horizontal bars, parallel bars, rings, and floor. In each event, competitors have to perform both compulsory and optional sequences on the apparatus. Compulsory exercises are set for four year periods and always include similar activities but in varying combinations. The exercises in this chapter are those chosen for competitors in the Olympics held in Montreal in 1976.

Olga Korbut, Russian Olympic
Gold Medalist 1972

There are three types of vault: the handstand, the horizontal vault, and vaults with turns. Of a team's twelve vaults, only four may be the same.

Each vault is divided into two sections—first and second flight. In the first flight, judges pay special attention to the take-off, including position and lift of body and its path through the air, and to the position of the body as it arrives on the horse. In the second flight, balance (in flight and on the floor), stretch of body, descent and general direction are most important. Competitors must place their hands on the horse as they perform their vaults.

1

In both the compulsory and optional exercises, two vaults may be performed: points for the better of the two are recorded.
In the optional exercises the two vaults may differ.
Competitors may make one supplementary run for the two vaults without penalty, provided they do not touch the horse.

compulsory vault
The compulsory exercise
selected for 1976 is known as
the Yamashita vault (above).
The horse must be turned
sideways.

1 With body and arms
outstretched,
2 jump onto horse
3 move forward into piked
position while leaving horse
and
4 straighten body,
5 landing with back to horse.

The maximum length allowed for the approach is 20 meters (66 feet). Competitors may choose how far to place the springboard from the horse. The approach is not scored.

Pre-flight is the time between take-off and the moment the gymnast's hands touch the horse.
One or both hands must be placed on the horse during the jump, at either the near or the far end, not in the center. The angle of the gymnast's body is very important. If he places his hands at the near end of the horse, his body must be in a horizontal position above the horse before his hands leave the horse.

The time between the gymnast's hands leaving the horse and the end of the flight is known as second flight. The height and length of the movement must produce the impression of a jump. From whichever end of the horse the gymnast jumps, his buttocks must rise $\frac{4}{5}$ of its height above it. His body should be vertical before he lands, $1\frac{1}{4}$ times the horse's length away from the horse if he has vaulted from the far end, or the horse's length if from the near end. The direction of flight must follow the length of the horse.

compulsory vault
The compulsory vault selected
for the 1976 Olympics is a
stoop vault with the hands
placed on the near end of the
horse.
The second flight takes place
as already described.

Points that the judges will look for include sureness of acrobatics, turns, and balances; full movements; general posture of body; co-ordination; lightness; and suppleness and relaxation.

The mat on which the gymnast performs must be 12 meters by 12 (about 40 feet by 40), and she must use the whole area, but without letting her feet go off the edge. Time allowed for the exercises is between one and one and a half minutes.

The musical accompaniment (on one instrument only) contributes to the overall effect of the exercises. It should not be too loud and must end in a logical way with the exercise.

Competitors must combine optional exercises with the compulsory exercises laid down for each event. The optional sequences devised by the gymnast must be varied and original and suit her build and temperament. They usually consist of a series of tumbles, together with jumps, spins, pirouettes, dance steps, and rolling, lying, and kneeling positions. All these are put together in such a way that she can display both gymnastic ability and genuine artistry.

1　　2　　3　　4

6　　7　　8　　9

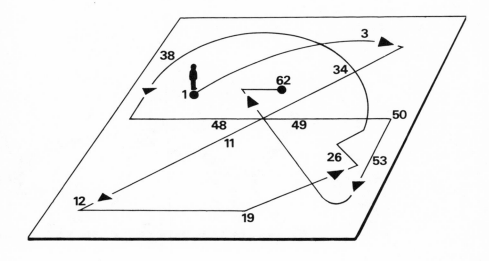

5

compulsory exercises
1 step forward with right foot;
2 step forward with left foot;
3 step obliquely forward with right foot and make full turn to right;
4 lean holding left leg to rear;
5 leap and cabriole;

10

6 lunge to right;
7 take two steps forward and make full turn with right leg $\frac{1}{2}$ bent;
8 step onto ball of left foot and
9 make $\frac{1}{4}$ turn to left;
10 make another $\frac{1}{4}$ turn to left and do hurdle jump;

11 round off jump and then execute 2 flic-flacs; step out and make $\frac{1}{2}$ turn to right; then do front handspring and step out again.

11

12 chasse forward;
13 step and develop;
14 rise on ball of right foot and
15 take 1 step to left;
16 cross legs and make $\frac{3}{4}$ turn to left;
17 step backward with arms raised;

12   13

18 step back and do cat leap backward onto left foot;
19 step back and make $\frac{1}{4}$ turn to left and jump up with legs apart;
20 step across and make $\frac{3}{8}$ turn to left;
21 swing right leg sideways and
22 turn cartwheel to right;
23 step to side and make $\frac{1}{4}$ turn to left;

18   19

14   15   16   17

20   21   22   23

24   25   26

28   29

32   33   34   35   36

24 turn $\frac{1}{2}$ circle with left leg;
25 place weight on left leg and
26 turn cartwheel to handstand position; make $\frac{1}{2}$ turn to left, finishing in kneeling position;
27 straighten body, make $\frac{1}{2}$ turn to right on left knee, and slide into front split;

27

28 make $\frac{1}{4}$ turn to left and execute stomach roll, finishing lying on front;
29 roll over on left side and lie on back;
30 raise left leg and
31 raise body to sitting position;

30   **31**

32 make $\frac{1}{8}$ turn onto left knee and
33 stand on right foot;
34 run into stag leap and
35 chasse left and right;
36 step to left and execute fish hop;
37 take 3 running steps

37

38 execute dive handspring,
and step out;
39 step to left and make ½ turn
to right;
40 lunge on right leg;

38

41 hop and make ¼ turn to left;
42 side lunge to right and
make ¼ turn to right on right
leg;
43 step forward on left leg and
turn ½ circle with right leg;
44 step forward on right leg
and turn ½ circle with left leg;
45 step to left;
46 step to right and make ½
turn to left;
47 step back and hop forward;

41   42   43

48 step back and make ¼ turn
to left;
49 chasse sideways, stepping
left with ¼ turn to left;
50 swing left leg forward and ½
turn to left,
51 landing with right leg
slightly bent;
52 make ¼ turn to left on right
foot;

48   49   50

39   40

44   45   46   47

51   52

53

55   **56**   **57**

58

53 step and tinsica forward and
54 take 2 steps forward;

55 step forward on right foot
and turn $\frac{3}{8}$ to right on right
foot;
56 step forward quickly and
57 take hurdle step into dive
cartwheel with $\frac{1}{4}$ turn back;
take 2 mounter flip-flops into
lunge;

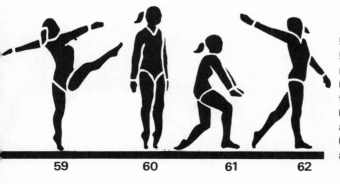

58 take cross step to left and
59 swing right leg sideways,
rising onto ball of left foot;
60 turn $\frac{1}{8}$ to left and chasse
forward;
61 place weight on right leg
and stretch left leg back;
62 stretch legs, swing right arm
and follow with head.

The optional floor exercises selected by competitors should be harmonious and rhythmical and express the gymnast's personality. He must include skips, jumps, handsprings, and saltos and must put the various movements together in a smooth and logical sequence, using the whole floor space.

The judges look for (a) flexibility, balance, hold, and strength, (b) and also creativity and imagination. They deduct points for over-long runs, lack of height and if any elementary movements of the gymnast's trunk and limbs are incorrect.

1

2

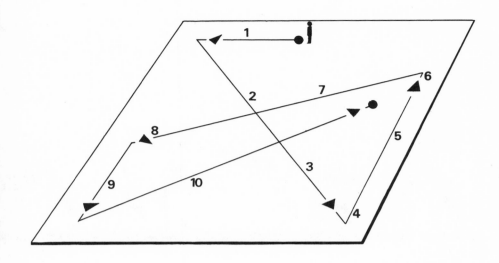

compulsory exercises
1 execute jump turn;

2 do handspring into front
tucked somersault;

3

4

3 do 2 headsprings;

4 cartwheel into arabesque;
5 make $\frac{1}{4}$ turn to left; do arab
spring leading into side
somersault;

5

6 circle left leg and do handstand; roll forward;

6

7 do cartwheel, then handspring, and fall to prone position;

7

8 push body up to handstand;
9 straddle down and roll
backward through to
handstand; turn and execute
cabriole jump turn;

8

9

10 run into arab spring; do 2
flic-flacs leading into back
tucked somersault.

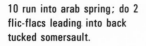

10

In these exercises the gymnast is judged on: her swinging movements; the passage of her body between the bars; the different hand grips she employs on each bar; her suspension; and the particularly difficult movements she includes in her sequence.

The exercises should be continuous, and the gymnast may only remain static for a moment. However, two pauses are allowed to regain balance and concentration, and if a gymnast falls she may resume within 30 seconds.

Competitors may only dismount from a hand-grasp, not by a somersault from the lower bar. Only two gymnasts from any one team may use identical mounts and dismounts.

compulsory exercises
1 after a short run, leap and place hands on low bar; straddle over low bar and hang momentarily stretched out from high bar;

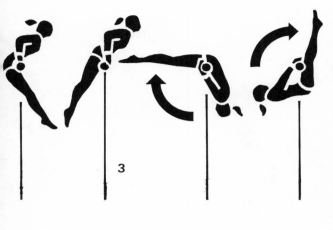

2 kip to front support on high bar;

3 roll forward and then swing backward to front lying position with hand on low bar;

4 cast legs backward, straddle over low bar, and execute stretched $\frac{1}{2}$ turn on high bar;

5 release grip and jump, grasping low bar and closing legs; do forward glide kip on low bar, releasing hands immediately and grasping high bar; hang backward from high bar; lift legs and hang backward from high bar over low bar;

6 kip to high bar;

7 roll forward and stand to support;

8 swing body and legs above bar;

9 swing forward and turn backward on low bar; execute Hecht dismount over low bar and finish exercise standing with back to bars.

8

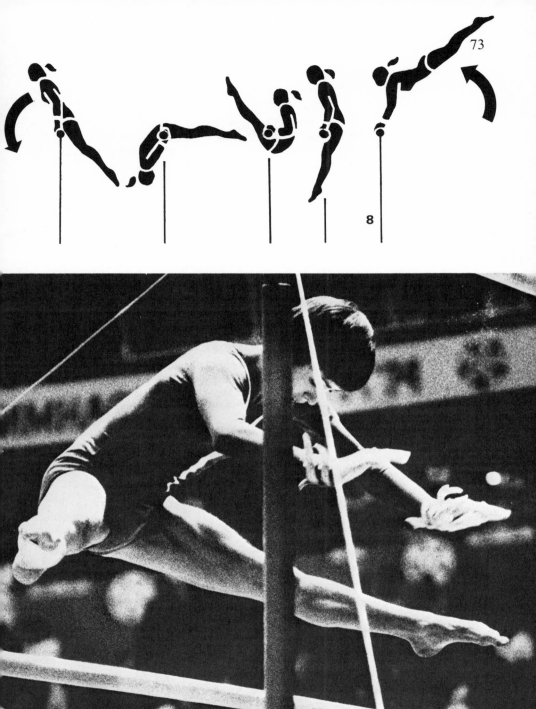

In his optional exercises the competitor must include forward and backward giant swings, as well as other movements, such as free hip-circles and turns. He must also make use of a variety of hand grips on the bar and must swing the whole time without stopping.

To have a chance of gaining maximum score, the gymnast must execute at least one movement in which he lets go of the bar with both hands simultaneously and grasps it again, also with both hands at the same moment.

compulsory exercises
1 jump up and hang from bar with reverse grip; propel body up toward handstand;
2 swing up and back and place feet between hands on bar; circle bar;

3 lift legs to handstand; take giant swing forward, changing left hand to regular grip; then make $\frac{1}{2}$ turn to left, swinging through hang in mixed grip;
4 on upward swing, vault over bar, making $\frac{1}{4}$ turn; grasp bar again in hanging position, swinging forward in regular grip;

5 squat with legs between hands; extend body backward and swing forward with body hanging extended;

6 extend body with hands gripping bar; circle backward and disengage legs, swinging forward and turning ½ to left; swing forward with mixed grips, finishing swing with both hands in reverse grip;

7 kip to handstand, immediately turning ½ left and forward to handstand;

8 giant swing backward;

9 on second giant swing backward, make ½ turn in giant swing forward (direct change);

10 take another giant swing forward; fall over and execute Hechtstraddle dismount over bar.

These exercises are intended to test the gymnast's balance. She must distribute the particularly difficult parts of her optional exercises logically, using the whole length of the beam. She should avoid too many lying and sitting positions and must include displays of balance, large and small turns, jumps and leaps, running and walking steps.

The exercise lasts between 80 and 105 seconds. Timing starts when the competitor's feet leave the floor and ends when they touch it again. Three stops are allowed, and if she falls she may resume within ten seconds.

Only two gymnasts from any one team may use identical mounts or dismounts.

compulsory exercises

1 run 2 or 3 steps forward from start and making $\frac{1}{2}$ turn leap to riding position;

2 rise to squatting position;

3 rise to ballet stand, making $\frac{1}{2}$ turn;

4 take 3 steps forward and

5 hop on left foot;

6 adopt ballet position;

7 step forward and make $\frac{1}{2}$ turn; do one-arm cartwheel, $\frac{1}{4}$ turn and lunge;

8 step forward, make $\frac{1}{2}$ turn and

9 sink to low squat;

10 stand with legs slightly bent;

11 step to left and jump down to squatting position;

4   5   6   7

9   10   11

12 make ½ turn to left, standing straight up at same time;

13 step forward; leap, putting weight onto other foot, and leap again;

14 hop and swing leg into step position;

15 make ¼ turn to left, then ½ turn to left and stand in straddled position;

16 lunge to side, make ¼ turn to right and stand with one leg raised behind;

17 step forward, swinging other leg, and lunge momentarily;

18 stand in ballet position and, swinging left leg, make full turn to right;

19 step forward and make ½ turn to left;

20 step forward, leap, run, and make ½ turn left to ballet stand;

21 cross legs; execute ballet stand facing left and raise right leg in front;

22 bend left leg ½ way;

23 take 2 steps forward and take stag leap;

24 step forward and ½ bend left leg;

25 do ballet stand, turning ½ to right;

26 step forward into handstand and lower right leg to beam;

27 putting weight onto left leg, make ¼ turn to left into sidestand;

28 make ¼ turn to right;

29 take 2 or 3 steps forward; turn layout somersault forward, making ½ turn; finish exercise by standing face forward.

12 13

16 17

22 23

28 29

14

15

18

19

20

21

24

25

26

27

The optional exercises on the parallel bars must include both swings and holds and should be so chosen that the gymnast can display his strength. Swinging and flight movements should predominate.

The exercises in the team competition must feature an especially difficult movement, executed under or over the bars, in which the gymnast releases both his hands from the bars at the same moment and grips them again simultaneously. In the combined and individual events, the competitors must release their grips both under and over the bars. The dismount must be in line with the overall difficulty of the routine. Handstands must be held for one second.

compulsory exercises
1 stand between bars and felge to position supporting hands between bars;

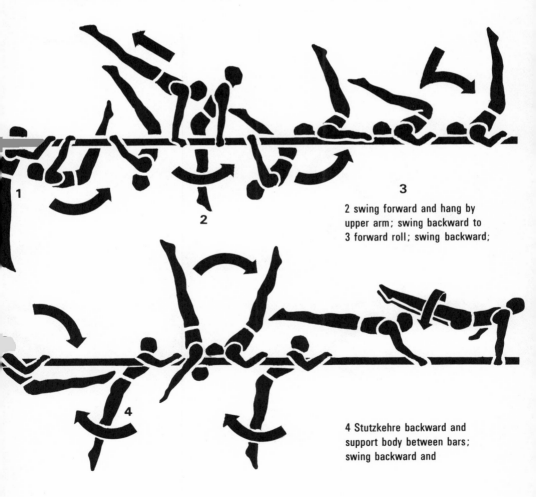

2 swing forward and hang by upper arm; swing backward to 3 forward roll; swing backward;

4 Stutzkehre backward and support body between bars; swing backward and

5 6

8 9

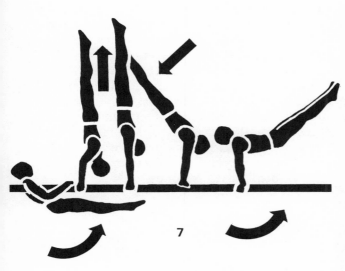

5 pirouette forward through handstand, immediately
6 descending to upper arms; swing forward and do backward roll through handstand position;
7 Stutzkehre forward into forward swing (of at least 30 degrees), hanging from upper arm;
8 execute front uprise to cross support position and
9 swing backward; straddle forward into 'L'-shaped position and hold;
10 press on bars with body bent, straight arms and legs together into handstand and hold;
11 salto backward without using hands and stand facing bars.

7

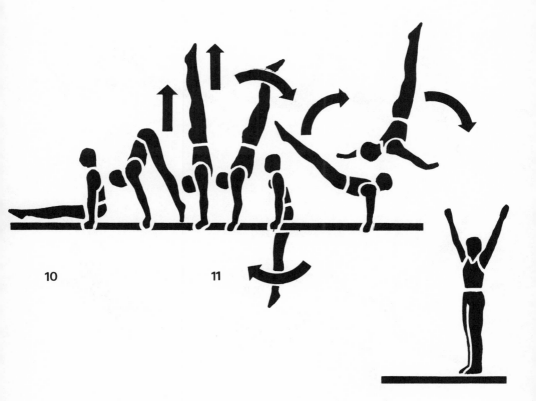

10   11

compulsory exercises

1 hang from the rings and bring legs forward to kip position; dislocate backward;

2 felge to handstand and hold;

3 fall backward through hang; execute giant dislocate backward through hang;

4 with straight arms execute front uprise to 'L'-shaped position and hold;

The competitor must demonstrate his ability to swing and to hold in his optional exercises, as well as displaying his strength. He must include at least two handstands, one of which should be designed to prove his strength; the other must be started from a hanging, inverted hanging, or supporting position. He must also display his strength with a movement as difficult as the other elements of the exercise. The rings must not be swung. The dismount must be in line with the overall difficulty of the routine. Handstands must be held for two seconds.

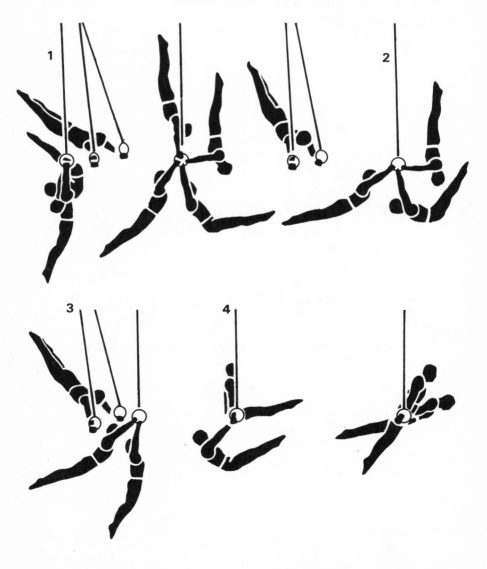

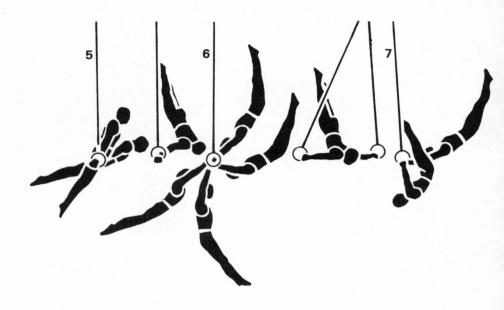

5 keeping body straight, bend arms and press up to handstand and hold;

6 fall forward through hanging position; execute high inlocate with straight body;

7 swing downward and inlocate to inverted hang with straight body; immediately bend body to kip position and kip;

8 lower body to position between rings and hold;

9 turn forward to inverted hang with straight body; swing down and back and execute back uprise; fall back to kip position;

10 dislocate backward; salto backward, bending and straightening body, to standing position.

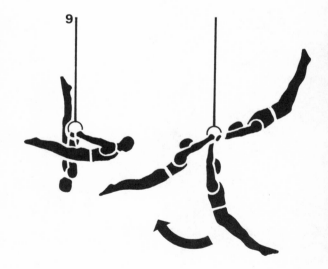

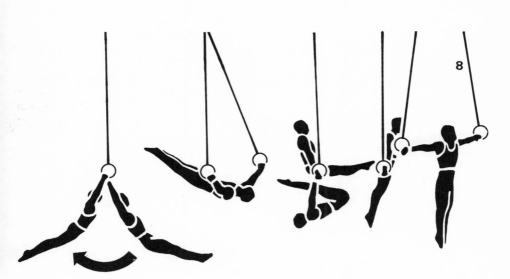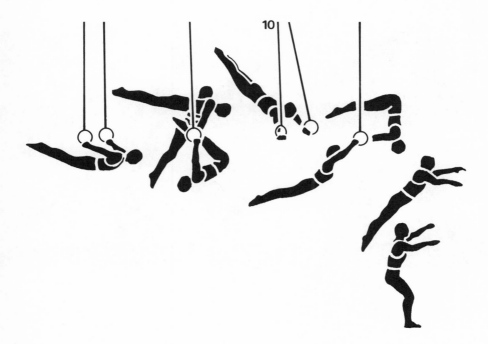

The competitor's optional exercises must be composed of clean swings without stops and must use all parts of the horse. Double leg swings should predominate, and the exercises should include: undercuts of one leg; circles of one and of both legs; and forward and reverse scissors, at least one of which must be executed twice in succession. The dismount must be in line with the overall difficulty of the routine.

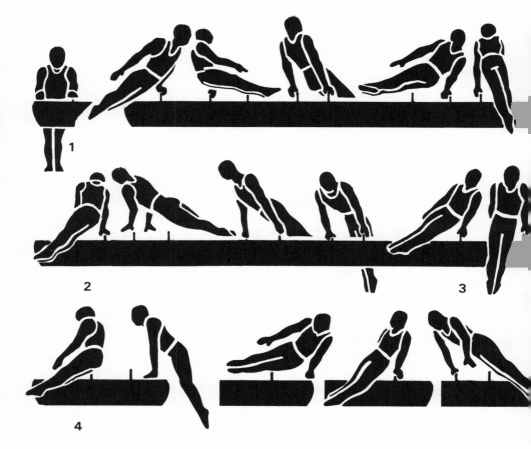

compulsory exercises
1 from starting position standing at side of horse, kehre in and circle horse with both legs $2\frac{1}{2}$ times;
2 execute double front vault (Double Swiss);
3 do double leg circle and kehre out;
4 travel sideways along length of horse into saddle;

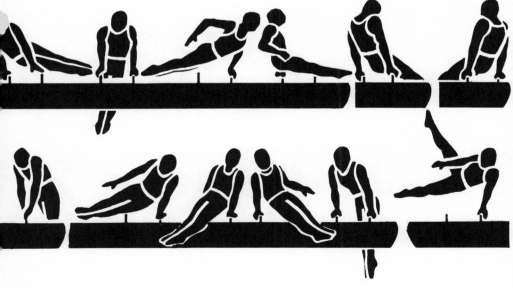

5 undercut and do backward scissors;

6 circle right leg backward and do 2 clockwise circles;

7 circle left leg forward and do 2 front scissors;

8 circle right leg forward and do 1 circle of horse with both legs;

9 travel off end of horse and kehre in again; circle horse twice;

10 do double front vault and dismount.

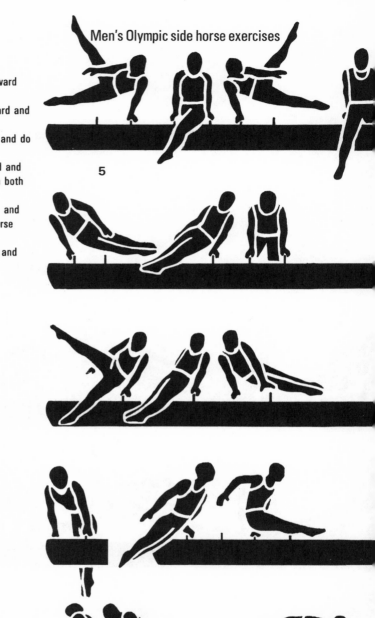

5

10

6

7

8

9

The judging of all gymnastic events, and especially those at international and Olympic levels, is organized very rigorously. Precise rules are laid down for the selection of judges and for the way in which they work. These ensure that the performers are judged as fairly as possible; in addition the rules are so detailed that it is almost impossible for any bias, whether accidental or deliberate, to go undetected.

Judges must have outstanding knowledge of and technical ability in gymnastics; they must also be known to be completely objective. Normally the corps of judges at a meeting is made up of one representative of each nationality taking part.

In major competitions, a superior judge and four other judges are appointed for each event. The superior judge is in charge and oversees the work of other judges. Some exercises require additional judges: they act as line or time judges or check that the compulsory exercises are done correctly. Such additional judges do not mark the competitors: their job is to signal if a rule has been broken.

Compulsory exercises are marked on a scale ranging from 0 to 10. The final score is obtained by taking the average of the two middle scores of the four judges. (For example, if the judges give scores of 7·1, 7·4, 7·6, and 8·0, then the scores of 7·1 and 8·0 are ignored. The final score is 7·4 +

A good coach ensures that the young gymnast learns proper technique from the first.

7·6 ÷ 2 = 7·5.) Out of the 10 possible points, 4 points are awarded for content, 6 for execution. For content, the marks are awarded as follows:

2 for exactness and correctness of exercise;

1·5 for exactness of rhythm;

0·5 for exactness of movement on floor.

For execution, the breakdown is:

1·5 for amplitude of movement;

1·5 for sureness of execution;

1 for elegance;

1 for coordination;

1 for lightness.

Detailed regulations lay down how many tenths of a point a judge may deduct for specific faults within each of these categories.

Similarly, between 0 and 10 points may be awarded for the optional exercises. Up to 6 points are allotted for the composition of the exercise:

4 for the difficult elements included;

1·5 for amplitude;

0·5 for general impression.

Of the 4 points awarded for execution:

1·5 are given for technical ability;

1·5 for amplitude;

1 for general impression.

Detailed regulations specify how every single aspect of the optional exercises should be marked.

As we have seen on the previous two pages, official judging is surrounded by rules and regulations, for judges must be fair and must also be seen to be fair. But how can we judge a gymnast ourselves, sitting in front of the television or, with luck, in a stadium watching an actual competition?

Top-class gymnasts are liable to the same faults as beginners at home and school, so look out for points mentioned elsewhere in this book. Most experienced gymnasts rarely make basic mistakes, but even the most famous do from time to time; watching them perform will help you to learn how the exercises should be performed.

The list below summarises the general faults for which judges have to watch. Use it to check the performance of professional gymnasts and, of course, your own as well!

Small faults—0·1 to 0·2 points deducted:
head or toes incorrectly positioned;
arms, legs, or body bending slightly;
legs straddling slightly (up to 45°);
landing without suppleness;
touching lightly with one or both feet;
slight loss of balance on landing;
slight hand support when not permitted;

tumbling
A poor back handspring:
1 take-off from balanced position;
2 head thrown back;
3 knees bent, hips not in lead;
4 bent vertical position with no balance; and
5 a heavy landing, head down.

1   2   3   4   5

slight faults in rhythm;
slight lack of amplitude.
Medium faults—0·3 to 0·4 points deducted:
arms, body, or legs definitely bending;
legs straddling (45–90°);
excessive body or arm movement to retain balance;
obvious lack of continuity between movements;
extra leg support on side of beam;
undesirable alternate hand placement.
Serious faults—more than 0·5 points deducted:
legs, arms, or body bending severely;
legs straddling more than 90°;
extra support with fingers, hands, or body when not permitted;
jerkiness;
serious lack of amplitude throughout exercise.
Points will also be deducted if the gymnast falls, or if she is caught, helped, or intentionally touched by her coach. In addition, a gymnast will be faulted if she breaks the restrictions on the time or area of her exercise, or if her attire or general conduct (or that of her coach) are unsatisfactory.

A good back handspring:
1 start in off-balance position;
2 head not in lead;
3 head stays between arms while hips lead;
4 straight vertical position as hands touch floor; and
5 light, balanced landing with head up.

1   2   3   4   5

asymmetrical bars

A poor forward seat circle,
catching high bar:
1 sitting on bar, knees not
above hands;
2 body touching bar during
circle;
3 rising with arched body; and
4 body bent on reach.

dance

A poor split leap:
1 support foot is half off floor,
body is behind it, head is
thrust forward;
2 weak leg thrust, back arched,
arms flying, shoulders high;
and
3 legs bent, body tilted back,
rear leg not turned out.

A good forward seat circle:
1 hips lifted high above bar
and knees above hands;
2 body piked and clear of bar;
3 rising in V position, almost
clear of bar; and
4 body straight on reach.

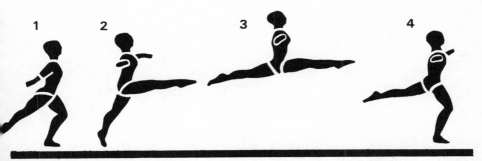

A good split leap:
1 support foot flat on floor,
body upright above it, head up;
2 take off from toes, back
straight, arms controlled,
shoulders relaxed;
3 legs straight, rear leg turned
out; and
4 weight over landing foot, rear
leg straight back.

A mass demonstration of
gymnastics in Berne, Switzerland.

Gymnastique moderne, which originated in France, is a branch of competitive gymnastics performed only by women. Though the sport has not yet been admitted to the Olympics, a world championship is organized every two years and takes place in odd-numbered years.

The emphasis in gymnastique moderne is on grace and beauty of movement. The exercises are performed with various kinds of hand apparatus, including ribbon, ball, two skittles, rope, hoolahoop, over a floor area measuring 12 meters by 12. Two such areas must be available, one covered by a thin mat, and competitors may choose between them. The exercises must last between 90 and 120 seconds.

Gymnasts compete both individually and in national teams of six. Teams perform compulsory exercises only—though the mirror image of the exercise may be performed, individual parts may not be changed. In the events for individual competitors, by contrast, the gymnast performs her own free style exercises as well as those laid down compulsorily.

The judges in gymnastique moderne events look for precision of movement and direction, rhythm, elegance, coordination, and musical and artistic interpretation. In the voluntary exercises they also keep a special watch for the complexity and originality of the gymnast's performance.

Beautiful curves and swirls of the ribbon, as the performer combines movement with poise.

Gymnastique moderne exercises

Exercises with a band.

Trampolining helps to condition the body for the more difficult gymnastic exercises and to develop balance, rhythm, co-ordination, timing, and endurance—all vital if you want to be a good gymnast.

Take care the first few times you go on the trampoline: it is so enjoyable that it is easy to forget about safety precautions and do yourself harm. Don't leap on or off the trampoline. Start by bouncing gently, just to get the feel of things. Then go on to the more difficult exercises, mastering one before you start another.

You should always have four people to watch you while you exercise. Called spotters, they warn you if you jump too close to the edge and are ready to catch you if necessary. Spotters are even allowed in official competitions.

basic movements
Stand with legs slightly apart, hands by sides. As you jump, swing arms above head, bringing feet together. As you descend, bring arms to sides and open legs, keeping them slightly bent.
To stop, bend knees as soon as you land and keep them well bent. Force heels down. Balance yourself by stretching arms out.

tuck bounce
Jump, bringing knees close up to chest and grabbing shins. As you descend, straighten up so that you land in standing position.

The trampoline is a sheet of woven webbing or heavy canvas about 12 ft. by 8 ft. stretched across a metal frame of about table height. Pads covering the edges of the frame are essential safety features.

pike bounce (left)
As you jump, lift legs together until parallel with trampoline, stretching arms out to touch ankles. Land in normal standing position.

half pirouette (right)
Bounce, do $\frac{1}{2}$ twist in air and land facing opposite direction. To start the twist, look over one shoulder, and bring other arm across stomach..

knee drop

As you descend from bounce,
bend knees so that you land on
them. Bounce back to standing
position. Keep back straight
and don't sit on heels.

seat drop

Take off as usual. At top of
bounce, raise legs and bend
back slightly so that you sit in
air. Land in sitting position,
with hands on bed behind hips.
Bounce back onto feet.

front drop

As you jump, lean forward and
lift legs back and up, so that
you land flat, elbows bent
slightly sideways. Hands, arms,
stomach, and thighs should all
hit trampoline at same moment.
Bounce to standing position
again.

back drop

Bounce and lean back as you
descend so that you land on
back, arms stretching out
sideways and feet extending
straight up. Then bounce back
onto feet.

swivel hips

Do seat drop. As you bounce up
from sitting position, swing
head and shoulders sideways,
executing a $\frac{1}{2}$ twist and
bringing legs through a
standing position in the air. Lift
legs and land in sitting
position, facing opposite
direction.

half turntable

Do front drop. As you bounce
up again, press hands sideways
on trampoline and, as body
turns, move into tucked
position. Keep back parallel to
trampoline. As you finish, turn,
release feet and land in front
drop position, facing opposite
direction from 1st drop.

111

half twist to front drop
Bounce. At top of bounce, look
over one shoulder, letting that
shoulder move backward. Then
lift legs up and back while
rotating shoulders forward.
Land in front drop position.
Return to feet.

half twist to back drop
Bounce. On ascent, start to
lean into front drop; but at top
of bounce, twist in air, as in
half pirouette. Land in back
drop.

There are trampolining competitions for individuals, teams of five, and synchronized pairs (performing on two parallel trampolines 2 m apart). All these include 10 compulsory and 10 voluntary routines. Marks are awarded for execution and difficulty, and deductions made for form breaks, loss of rhythm and height, and lack of synchronization.

The trampoline beds must be of the woven kind. Floor mats must surround the trampoline on all sides.
Sports shirts and long gymnastic trousers are worn by men, and leotards by women. Both must wear trampoline shoes. Spotters must wear training suits.
There are 9 officials present for judging the trampolining: 1 referee, 4 judges for execution, 2 for difficulty, and 2 for synchronized jumping. There are also chief recorders, assistants, and an arbitration jury.
Spotters must not speak to competitors. If they do, 0.3 of a mark is deducted each time.

individual competitions
The ten best competitors in a preliminary round go forward to a final round. The preliminary round consists of 1 compulsory and 1 voluntary routine, and the final 1 voluntary routine.

team competitions
There are 5 members in a team, and all perform 1 compulsory and 2 voluntary routines. Team scores are made by adding the 4 best scores for each routine.

synchronized competitions
Pairs of competitors jump the same routine simultaneously. Competitions consist of 1 compulsory and 1 voluntary routine, the compulsory being the same as for individual competitions. Each competitor may start in only one pair.

The illustrations opposite and below show some advanced trampoline routines.

the routines
Each routine, whether compulsory or voluntary, consists of 10 movements. You can only have a 2nd attempt at either if the jury decides that you were disturbed eg by the spectators or by a faulty trampoline.

competition cards
You must enter the details of your voluntary routines on a competition card and give it to the referee two hours before the competition. Entries are checked by the judges of difficulty. You are still allowed to change the order of your routines.

warming up
You are allowed two hours training before the start of the competition, and also one practice routine before each round for which you have qualified.

start
Once you are on the trampoline, the referee signals the start. You can make as many preliminary jumps as you want: scoring only starts with the first part of the actual routine.

interruption
An interrupted routine is only scored to the point of interruption.

end of a routine
You should land on your feet after the 10th movement, and may then jump once more in a stretched position. If you fail to land on your feet, you are judged as having made an extra movement, and 1 point is deducted. You must stand upright for at least 3 seconds after landing, or you lose another point.

The illustration below shows another advanced routine. The photograph opposite is of a young London trampoliner, who reached the UK national championship finals just by practicing after school.

marking for difficulty

Routines are marked in tenths of a point from 0.1 All jumps without rotation score no degree of difficulty.
Other jumps are rated:
90° somersault 0.1
360° somersault 0.4
180° twist 0.1
360° twist 0.2 points.
Twisting somersaults bring marks for both somersaulting and twisting. Piked and straight somersaults without twists score an extra 0.1 point for difficulty.

repeats

If you repeat a jump in the voluntary routine, there is no score for the degree of difficulty of the repeat. But multiple somersaults with twists in the first, middle, and last phase have the same degree of difficulty: they are regarded as different jumps, not repeats. Tucked, piked, or straight positions are also considered different jumps.

scoring

Of the execution judges' marks, the highest and lowest are removed and the other two are averaged. The recorder then makes deductions for mistakes in synchronization and doubles the result. The final score is obtained by adding the marks for difficulty and making deductions for interruptions.

result

The competitor or team with the highest total points wins. Competitors with equal marks in individual or synchronized competitions are given the same placing—except that when they tie for 1st place, a jump-off (a 3rd voluntary routine) is held. If a tie occurs in a team competition, all places are shared.

Ballet

You may not think that ballet has much to do with a successful gymnast winning a Gold Medal at the Olympic Games. In fact, the art and the sport are closely connected. They demand from those who take part the same kind of tough training and devotion, the same rhythm and balance, and the same tight control over the body. And the beauty of movement that all this produces is the same, whether you are watching gymnast or ballerina.

On this and the next seven pages we show some of the most important exercises for both dancer and gymnast. Without mastering them, there is no hope of success. With them there is a basis for success—but only a basis. Through her movements and the accompanying music, the dancer tells a story or expresses an emotion. The gymnast combines individual movements to demonstrate the pure beauty of supreme skill.

Correct posture is vital for the dancer. In the arabesque, shown above, the hip must be pressed down, the leg fully stretched and rotated; the body should lean forward. The shoulder and extended leg should be parallel to the floor.

The graceful and thrilling perfection of an international ballet star. Yet some world-famous dancers (such as Markova) began their careers on the advice of doctors—exercising so as to combat some slight physical handicap.

The five positions of the feet are the basis of all steps in classical dance and of the beauty and precision of the great ballerinas.

These foot positions are all based on a turning outward of the legs, from the hips right down to the feet. This gives beauty of body line and improves balance. It is very important and has to be practiced endlessly.

A dancer's arms add grace and beauty to her movements. The five positions of the arms in classical dance, shown below, form a circle.

Ballet

Ballet dancers exercise their body muscles on a barre, a wooden rail running around the edge of their rehearsal room. These exercises, some of which are illustrated on this and the next five pages, take up at least half an hour at the beginning of each training session or class. They condition the dancer's body so that it is able to fulfil the enormous physical demands made on it.

You can try these exercises at home, using a table-edge, window sill, or door-knob, instead of the barre. Remember to do them facing both ways so that you exercise both sides of your body.

pliés (left)
Stand sideways by barre and grasp it with one hand. Bend knees, being careful not to roll ankles inward. Keep back straight and hips tucked under. After maximum bend, return to stand and then rise on points.

To come up press heels into floor and straighten up. Count 4 while bending, 4 while returning to stand, 4 on points, and 4 while returning to stand again.

battement fondu (below)
These movements, which guide
the body from a relaxed
position to a full stretch and
back to a relaxed position,
train the dancer to descend
from a jump.

port de bras (left)
This exercise develops circular
movements of arms and of the
whole body. It is later used for
contractions and suppling
movements.

stretching exercises (left and
below)
These exercises are intended to
keep the muscles and ligaments
in condition. Do them carefully
and don't try to push your body
too far.

After warming up at the barre, the dancer starts work on the floor of the rehearsal room. This is known as center practice. The exercises devised for this part of her training are intended to develop her poise and balance, so that she can move with grace and beauty, both on the stage and through the air.

A   B   C   D

grand battement, devant (a) and derrière (b). The leg is stretched out fully.

arabesque (c)
Raise leg and arms and stretch out parallel to floor. The support leg is straight, with chest and shoulders lifted.

brisé (d)
Holding one arm up, push off from points with both feet.

cat leap (left)
From demi-plié, swing leg forward, turning foot and knee out. Jump from back leg, lifting front foot up, with arms above head. Bring back leg forward and up as lead leg comes down, turning both feet out. Land on front leg in demi-plié.

split leap (above)
Take off from demi-plié, keeping support leg firmly on floor. Stretch front leg forward, keeping back straight, and stretch out back leg, heel upward. At top of leap, legs should be in a split position. Take bodyweight on front leg on landing, and finish in demi-plié.

stag leap
Push off from back leg, bending front leg at knee so that it just touches rear knee and pressing forward with arms. Stretch and turn out rear leg. Stretch front leg out so that body is in split position, twisting it sideways if desired. Land on front leg, keeping rear leg extended.
In all these exercises, do not lurch forward as you jump but lift the body with the legs in one movement.

cabriole (above)
May be done forward,
backward, or sideways. Step
onto left leg in demi-plié,
thrusting right leg into air,
parallel to ground, knee
straight and toes pointed. Then
left leg is thrust into air, to tap
against calf of right leg.
Landing is in demi-plié on left
leg.

jeté en tourant (below)
Run or slide into this jump so
that you thrust yourself into the
air. As you bring second leg up,
keep turning rapidly, lifting
arms above head and reaching
for floor with first leg. The
legs move through a scissors
motion. Hold second leg in
arabesque position and land in
demi-plié.

fouette (left)
Standing on points, fold arms in front of chest and raise left foot to right knee. Whip body around to face other way and then turn around again quickly, stretching left leg and right arm out and descending from points.

pirouette (above)
From demi-plié, begin to twist arms and body, moving weight onto front foot. Extend rear leg and, standing on points, turn front leg, taking bodyweight on front leg and leaning forward slightly. Keep the support leg straight.

turn in arabesque penchée (below)
Lunge deeply, moving body down and sideways, extending rear leg and straightening front leg. Stretch arms and rear leg and rotate on points of front foot. To complete exercise, lift body, maintaining bodyweight on ball of front foot.

It is clear that gymnastics isn't something exclusive, only for those who want to train for the big international competitions. The skills that we develop through regular gymnastic exercises (even if only for a few minutes a day at home) will help us in all our normal day-to-day activities, by ensuring better and more efficient use of the body.

If we look back into history, we find that gymnastics were in existence long before they were recognized as an official sport in 1896. Fred Astaire and Gene Kelley are as much gymnastic

Folk dancing ranges from Russian Cossack dancing to English Morris dancing and American square and round dancing.
Whatever their style, the dances have been handed down through generations.
Although they may have had their origins in religious ritual, for centuries they have been one of the most popular forms of social relaxation.

stars as Olga Korbut, and before them came a whole line of 'gymnasts'—bullfighters, circus artistes, medieval strolling players who could turn their hands to anything, bull-leapers such as those depicted on classical vases, and tribal dancers since the earliest days of man.

All the dance types shown on these pages demand gymnastic skills: rhythm, balance, careful control of the body. You don't have to be a gymnast to perform well on the dance floor, but it does help!

It was with ragtime in the 1910s and 1920s that informal 'pop' dancing started. It has continued ever since, through the Charleston, Rock n' Roll and the Twist to the latest fashions in the discotheques.

Ballroom dancing developed in the early part of this century and has remained popular ever since. Among the most famous dances are the waltz, veleta, two-step, tango, and cha-cha.

double Lutz jump

Ice figure skating is another sport that calls for gymnastic ability. There are three types of figure-skating competition: single skating, pair skating, and ice dancing. In each, competitors must perform compulsory movements and a selection of movements of their own choice. Performers are judged on their artistry and on their technical ability.

The exercises illustrated here are very similar to those performed in international gymnastics competitions. Of course, the most important difference is that they take place on ice and thus the gymnast's balancing ability becomes extra-important for the ice-skater.

Axel-Paulsen jump

sit spin

camel spin

(left)
forward dive

(right)
reverse dive

Like gymnastics, competitive diving demands
balance and strict body control. Divers may take
off from the board facing forward or backward
or from a handstand. Their flight may be straight,
piked, or tucked. The diver must enter the water
vertically or nearly so, with his body straight and
his toes pointed.

(left)
inward dive

(right)
twist dive

"Calisthenics" means exercises that use rhythmical movement, but little or no equipment, to produce strength and flexibility. Such exercises are practiced by individuals throughout the world; but in China group calisthenics are the basis of a daily national program of physical fitness.

"Promote physical culture and improve the people's health", said Chairman Mao, who realized the importance of physical fitness for the Chinese; and he devised a program of simple exercises that can be performed by anybody almost anywhere.

Every morning and twice during each day, a bugle sounds over loudspeakers throughout China, and people in all walks of life stop whatever they are doing and spend four minutes doing the physical fitness program. The exercises are valuable in that they are simple and systematic, stimulating but not too strenuous for the elderly or for those of poor health. They require no equipment nor a great deal of space; and during the four minutes the whole body is exercised in an enjoyable and relaxing way.

Calisthenics on the beach at Long Island, USA, earlier this century.

134

19th century circus gymnasts
demonstrate their agility and
contortionist's abilities.

Home exercises

Stand with arms to sides. Stretch arms backward and bend back, holding arms straight down. Bend forward slowly, bringing arms straight above head.
(Lower back; shoulders.)

So far we have described how you can start training to become a gymnast, and we have shown the exercises that have to be done in Olympic and other major competitions.

But gymnastics isn't a matter of working to become a star. It leads to something much more important: personal physical fitness. The old Latin phrase *mens sana in corpore sano*, a healthy mind in a healthy body, is still true today. Being fit doesn't just mean that you can run fast to catch a bus or stand on your head longer than a friend! It means looking after your body so that it functions properly. If it does, you will be able to work and play efficiently, and you will probably also be a happier person. Physical balance, described on this page and the next, leads to mental balance, to a balanced and stable personality.

It's a good idea to work out a program of daily exercises to do at home. They needn't take more than a few minutes, but you should do them regularly: violent exercise once a week will strain your body, five minutes a day will keep it fit. Gradually make your program a little more difficult, but never push yourself too far: if you master one new exercise a fortnight, or even one a month, you will be doing well. Above all, enjoy keeping fit!

Stand with arms to sides. Swing arms up until they make right angle with body, keeping them straight all the time.
(Shoulders.)

Sit cross-legged, with arms behind back, hands touching. Lift arms slowly, keeping back straight. (Shoulder girdle.)

Lie with arms by sides, resting chin on floor. Bend knees slowly, reach back and grasp feet. Then pull body and thighs forward and up, and hold for count of 10, breathing slowly. Lower slowly. (Lower back, seat, and thighs.)

From sitting position, lean forward and grasp knees. Bring knees toward chin, lean back and hold for 5 seconds. (Lower back.)

Lie flat with chin on floor and arms beneath shoulders. Slowly tilt head back and lift body, pressing hands on floor, until arms are straight and head back. Keep hips against floor. Return to prone position. (Arms, shoulders, seat, hips.)

Lie flat with chin on floor and arms stretched out together on floor beyond head. Contract lower back and seat, raising legs and body from floor. Hold, then return to starting position. (Seat, lower back, back of thighs.)

Sit on stool, with back straight and arms stretched out sideways. Then twist torso as far as possible in one direction. Return to forward-facing position, and then repeat to other side. Be careful not to twist hips. (Waist.)

Lie on stomach, keeping legs
straight, pointing toes and
placing hands on floor under
shoulders. Press on hands and
raise body, leaving knees and
feet on floor. Then lower body
slowly back toward floor—but
repeat push-up before floor is
actually touched. (Arms.)

Lie on floor as above. Lift body
from floor so that hands take
whole weight of body and
head. Body and legs should
form straight line. Then arch

the back by lifting the hips
and thrust head down to look
at knees. (Arms, lower back,
back of legs.)

Lie face down on floor as
above. Press hands into floor
and lift body, turning toward
left and supporting
bodyweight on right hand. Place
left hand on hip. Repeat
toward other direction. (Arms
and sides of body.)

Stand facing a wall, lean forward on toes and place hand on wall to support bodyweight. Remove hand and swing arms swiftly so that the other hand touches wall. Repeat rapidly. (Shoulders, stomach.)

Stand with legs apart and bend arms at shoulder level. Keeping upper part of arm still, rapidly circulate each forearm and hand, one clockwise, the other counter-clockwise. Repeat, moving entire arm. Then repeat with arms out straight. (Arms and shoulders.)

Stand straight, feet together and hands by sides. Lift first right then left knee as high as possible. Repeat exercise with hands on hips. (Stomach, thighs.)

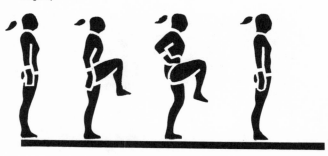

Stand with feet together and bend forward slowly, clasping hands behind knees. Then slide hands down back of legs to calves, bending head toward floor, and brace arms on floor. Don't bounce—hold steadily. (Lower back, backs of legs.)

Stand straight, with arms on hips. Keeping body upright and arms still, step forward and bend front leg, stretching out back leg. Return to standing position and repeat with other leg as fast as possible. (Legs.)

Crouch with body and head forward and arms stretched out. Press on feet and stand up straight, keeping arms stretched out at right angles to body. (Legs.)

Lie on left side, supporting head on left hand, pressing right hand palm-down into floor and keeping legs together. Lift right leg as high as possible, lower it, and then lift both legs together, pressing right hand into floor for support. Keep left leg and upper body in straight line – don't bend at hips. Do not let legs sway in air. Repeat exercise lying on right side. (Inside of thigh, hips.)

Stand with legs apart. Bend left leg, letting body move left and down. Return to starting position and repeat to right. Don't move fast, and don't let knee of straight leg turn toward floor. (Hips and thighs.)

Crouch with feet apart and hands clasped together behind head. Press legs into floor and jump, keeping legs and body straight and hands behind head. Descend to starting position and repeat. (Legs.)

Lie on floor, hands by sides and lower part of legs and feet tucked under body. Pressing hands into floor, raise body into sitting position. (Stomach, top of thighs.)

Lie flat on back, arms stretched out together behind head. Sit up, bending forward to reach toward feet. Do not let legs rise from floor. Lie back and repeat. (Stomach, upper legs.)

Lie flat on back, as before, but with knees bent and feet flat on floor. Sit up, letting arms go outside knees. Lie backward and repeat. (Stomach.)

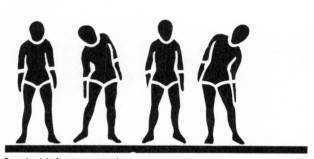

Stand with feet apart and hands to sides. Bend to one side from waist, stretching hand as far down leg as possible. Do not raise either leg off ground or move forward. Repeat for other side. (Waist.)

Stand with legs slightly apart and arms stretched out above head, hands clasped. Keeping legs and arms straight, swing body from side to side, continuing to clasp hands and keeping feet flat on floor. Don't let the body lean forward at the waist. (Waist.)

Stand with legs apart and arms fully stretched out sideways. Bend to left from waist, grasping calf with left hand and stretching right arm straight out. Do not bend knees. Repeat exercise bending to right. (Waist.)

Lie on back, arms straight by side, legs straight. Lift legs straight up so that they form right angle with body. Keep arms and body still and straight. Press lower back against floor throughout. (Stomach, legs.)

Stand with feet together and hands on hips. Bend body forward and roll and twist it to right, continuing in a complete circle so that body bends back and then rolls forward again from left. Repeat exercise in opposite direction. (Waist, lower back.)

This exercise should be done with the help of a partner, who holds your heels to the floor all the time.
Lie on back with legs about 12 inches apart and hands clasped behind head. Keeping legs straight and hands behind head, sit up, as you do so bending body so that left elbow touches right knee. Finish with straight body at right angles to feet. Repeat exercise in other direction. (Stomach, hips, upper legs.)

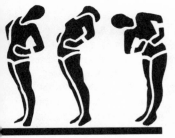

Lie on back, tuck knees to chest, arms stretched out sideways. Rotate legs to left, keeping shoulders on floor. Return to starting position and repeat to right. (Hips, waist.)

Lie on back, legs straight, arms stretched out sideways. Raise legs straight into air so that they form right angle with body. Then, keeping body straight, swing both legs first to left, then to right. (Hips, thighs, stomach.)

Many circus artistes are as skilled as the greatest gymnasts. Nor is gymnastics their only talent, for they, like everyone else who works in a circus, have to help with anything that needs to be done.

Try not to practice against a door. Choose a clear wall with no obstacles.

squat hand balance
Squat with hands flat on floor, arms between legs and knees above elbow. Lean forward onto hands and then lift toes off floor until you are balancing on hands. Keep head up and press fingers down to retain balance.

squat head balance
Squat as above, lean forward until head touches floor, and lift toes up.

handstand
With hands straight above head, step forward and bend front leg, keeping arms out in line with body. As hands reach toward floor, swing back leg up to vertical; when hands have reached floor, push up front leg. In final position, ankles are over hips, hips over shoulders, and shoulders over hands.

headstand

Squat, lean forward on hands, placing head on floor to form triangle with hands, and bending body at hips. Then push up to handstand position, arching back slightly to retain balance and tucking the hips under.

head and elbow balance

Do head balance, but place hands beside head and keep forearms flat on floor. Then kick up as already described.

forearm balance

Place forearms and hands on floor. Raise hips as high as possible by moving shoulders forward over elbows. Keep feet on floor, head up.

head balance

Squat. Then put head on floor about 10 inches in front of hands and 'walk' feet forward, raising hips and keeping weight on head. Kick up with one foot, keeping other on mat, and then push other leg up. Bring feet together, arching back, and supporting bodyweight on hands and head.

Poise is important for everyone. It is not only the gymnast who must achieve balance and control the movements of his body. In fact, poise is a matter of making the best use of our bodies and keeping them fit: standing, walking, and sitting properly aren't to be left to slightly prim old relations. If you are honest about it, you will soon notice how much more comfortable you become once your posture is correct.

With a book on your head stand straight, arms by sides. Then walk slowly forward, stretching your arms out sufficiently to retain balance. When you have mastered this, try to crouch, keeping the book on your head. Stretch your arms out sideways to maintain balance.

Stand on toes, feet together and palms touching above head. Slowly bend knees to squatting position, keeping hands on head and remaining on toes. Then stand up gently, lowering arms to sides.

Lie on back, legs straight, arms by sides. Press into floor with hands and lift legs, bending them over backward. As back straightens toward vertical, support body with hands, keeping elbows flat on floor and taking bodyweight on shoulders. To descend, bend legs and place hands on floor. Lower body to floor, straighten legs, and lower to starting position.

This is one of the basic Yoga positions. Sit cross-legged, pulling your ankles in as much as possible. The body should be erect but not tense, wrists resting on knees. Try to concentrate on something in front of you for a minute or so; push any other thoughts out of your mind.

Lie on back with feet straight and hands on floor at sides, palms upward. Close eyes and breathe slowly and quietly, so that the whole body relaxes.

Sit with feet and lower part of legs tucked together under upper legs. Bend forward until head touches floor, placing arms next to legs. Then let whole body relax.

Stand with feet together. Breathe out and relax so that body is limp. Breathe in deeply and stretch arms sideways, palms uppermost. Then bring hands together over head and stand on toes, stretching as high as possible. Hold and count to 5. Breathe out slowly and relax body, holding arms out to side.

Yoga originated in the East. Its keenest practitioners claim that it is a complete philosophy of life which makes it possible for every human being to understand his or her place in the world.

The kind of life we lead in the West means that not many people can take up this approach to life or even want to try. Despite this, it is quite easy to learn some of the more simple Yoga poses. These are designed to lead to greater physical flexibility, to do away with physical and mental strain, and to be first steps toward true mental relaxation.

Some of the poses shown on this page and the next three are similar to the ordinary gymnastic exercises already described. Don't think, however, that Yoga is just another way of keeping fit. It is far removed from the hectic competition and activity of the gymnasium. It involves the individual in trying to reach inner physical and mental calm.

The best thing to do is not to rely on the suggestions here but to get hold of a book on Yoga or better still to join a class in it.

When you try the poses, remember to do them very slowly and quietly, a few at a time. Put a towel or mat on the floor and wear loose clothing in which you feel comfortable.

Sit on knees with back straight and hands on knees. Lean forward slightly, stretch fingers, extend tongue as far as possible, widen eyes and stretch eye muscles. Hold for count of 5 and relax slowly.

Sit on knees and twist left arm behind back, palm out. Bring right arm over shoulder and grasp fingers of left hand. Pull arms in opposite directions.

Stand with feet apart, arms stretched sideways. Slide right hand down outside of leg and bring left arm horizontally above head. Do not bend forward or backward. Return to starting position and repeat on opposite side of body.

Sit with back and legs straight. Bend legs out, bringing soles together. Then grasp ankles and gently lower knees to floor. Hold for as long as is comfortable.

Sit with legs straight and hands on thighs. Bending body back slightly, raise arms and clasp hands above head. Bend forward slowly and grasp knees with hands, keeping back straight and knees firm. Holding knees, bend body forward with head toward knees and elbows bent out. Hold for count of 20.

Kneel with knees touching, head lowered, hands on floor and fingers stretched. Breathe in and out, lifting and pushing abdomen out. Repeat 5 times. As you breath in, body is contracted and back rounded; as you exhale, back arches.

Sit with legs straight, about 12 in. apart. Pull left foot in so that it rests against right thigh. Pull right foot into fold of left leg, place hands on knees and sit straight but not rigid. Attempt same exercise again, but pull left foot into fold of right.

Sit with legs straight. Twist right leg over left. Place right hand on floor behind body, grasp left knee with left hand and twist body as far to right as possible. Repeat exercise in opposite direction.

Lie on back, legs straight, hands on floor at sides, palms down. Lift legs upward and back over head until toes touch floor. Keep legs straight. To end the exercise, bend knees and bring them above head.

Roll body forward, keeping head and hands on floor. Straighten legs when hips touch floor. Lower legs to floor, keeping hands straight.

Sit up with legs crossed and hands clasped behind head. Bend body to right and touch right elbow with right knee; straighten and repeat to left.

Then twist body and touch right knee with left elbow, straighten and repeat to left.

Sit with legs straight. Stretch arms out, bend left leg and tuck into right. Swing arms up. Bend forward and grasp right ankle, keeping leg straight. Pull leg, bending arms gently. Swing arms over head and straighten body.

Some advanced Yoga postures.

amplitude   fullness of body movement in which body is always stretched to its full extent.

arabesque   body in profile, supported on one leg with other stretched back, one arm stretched sideways, the other stretched up.

arab spring   spring similar to cartwheel in which legs come together at vertical and body makes $\frac{1}{4}$ turn.

axis   line around which the body rotates.

battement fondu   a strong thrusting movement in ballet, usually a jump which is concluded with a soft landing.

battement derrière   strong backward leap.

battement devant   forward throwing movement of the body.

battement grand   characterized by a strong thrusting motion with high elevation or wide extension.

beatboard   apparatus used in vaulting exercises to give greater elevation to the jump.

bridge position   from a handstand position, move shoulders backward away from direction of fingers and bend body so that feet reach toward floor and are slightly apart on landing. Knees must bend to form a wide back arch.

brisé   basic ballet step in which the dancer pushes from two feet while brushing one foot into the air to rejoin them on landing.

cabriole   step in which legs are caught in air and thrown to further height before body descends to floor.

cat leap swing front leg up and forward, half bending it and turning it half out at the same time; jump off from back leg, swinging it in the same way so it passes descending front leg; land in demi-plie.

chassé kind of gallop in the air in which one foot chases the other but never passes it.

demi-plié heels on floor, ankles bent, bending knees and pushing them out over toes; hips should be flexible, but body should remain erect.

dislocate start from piked position on rings; thrust legs up and back while spreading arms out to sides and turning them at the same time; arch body and swing feet back down to touch the floor.

dislocate giant dislocate action as above but legs are thrust with greater force and the circle of body is wider.

dive handspring take a few running steps and 'dive' into handstand position; vigorously push off the floor with hands so that body turns over onto feet.

felge from forward swing in support, lower backward to inverted hang; turn backward letting go and re-grasping parallel bars in front or hang position.

fouette series of whipping turns performed on one spot.

front support hands on bar by hips, body straight with shoulders over hands for balance, heels lifted.

glide lying position in air with body straight, legs extended and arms by sides.

Hecht jump jump from higher of two asymmetrical bars through piked position, in which body is folded around lower bar, continuing to circle until legs point down at angle of 45°; then extend body from hips and jump to floor, keeping legs straight and extending arms.

inlocate have partner lift one of your legs up toward piked position; bring hips up toward the rings and bend head, turning arms inward so that you finish in a piked position.

jeté leap from one foot to the other.

jeté en tournant leaping motion from foot to foot while turning.

kip body in piked position, ankles to the bar. As hips move back under the bar, legs extend up and out, moving the hips up to the bar. The arms press down, rotating the upper body back up and around to front support.

mixed grip (bars) one hand in regular grip, the other in reverse.

piked position standard position for performing various exercises where the knees are straight and the hips flexed as much as possible.

pirouette full turn on one foot giving impression of rapid spring.

plié	as demi-plié, but knees should be bent and be held bent for longer.
port de bras	carriage and movement of the arms.
regular grip (bars)	hands placed on top of bars, fingers facing away from body; also known as ordinary grip.
reverse grip (bars)	hands placed under bar, with fingers behind bar.
salto	a complete 360° rotation of the body from feet to feet or hands to hands or on the apparatus.
split leap	jump from both feet into air, high enough to allow legs to stretch as far apart as possible; lean body slightly forward.
stag leap	bring legs up quickly, bending front one and keeping back one straight, at same time extending arms horizontally.
straddle	position of body with legs apart.
tinsica	lean toward floor with body and arms and push off with one leg, hands touching floor one after another; as first hand leaves floor, first foot reaches it; push off from floor with second hand, lifting and arching body and stretching second leg out to retain balance.
tuck	position of body with back rounded, chin on chest, knees bent up to chest.